BOB MARLEY

A Life from Beginning to End

Copyright © 2021 by Hourly History.

All rights reserved.

The cover photo is a derivative of "Bob Marley" (https://commons.wikimedia.org/wiki/File:Bob-Marley-in-Concert_Zurich_05-30-80_cropped.jpg) by Ueli Frey, used under CC BY-SA 3.0 (https://creativecommons.org/licenses/by-sa/3.0/deed.en) and "Bob Marley" (https://commons.wikimedia.org/wiki/File:Bob_marley_01.jpg) by Paul Weinberg, used under CC BY-SA 3.0 (https://creativecommons.org/licenses/by-sa/3.0/deed.en)

Table of Contents

Introduction
From Farm to Trench Town
Marley's First Songs
Topping the Charts in Jamaica
Marriage and Children
Marley the Rastafari
The Birth of Reggae Music
Commercial Success
The Wailers Break Up
No Woman, No Cry
The Assassination Attempt
Conclusion
Bibliography

Introduction

Robert Nesta "Bob" Marley was the son of a British Jamaican by the name of Norval Sinclair Marley and a native Jamaican mother, Cedella Malcolm. Bob's father is said to have been a captain in the British Royal Marines, but he met Cedella on her father Omeriah Malcolm's farm in Nine Mile. It remains unclear exactly how Norval ended up on the Malcolm farm, but it appears he came into contact with the family during his work as an overseer in the region.

After a quick courtship, Norval married Cedella on June 9, 1944. The couple stood out from the beginning. Interracial marriages were rare in the 1940s to be sure, but what really made them unusual was their age gap. Cedella was only 18 years old at the time, whereas Norval was nearly 60. Details as to the nature of their relationship are scarce. Some anecdotal tales speak of how the two would run into each other while Norval was renting a house nearby the Malcolm farm.

The relationship seems to have begun innocently enough with the older man playfully joking with the girl, but it wasn't long before the little jokes they shared blossomed into a full-blown romance. Sadly though, whatever passion had existed between the two seems to have been short-lived. Shortly after their marriage, Norval announced that he had marching orders to go to Kingston, Jamaica's capital.

After his departure, Norval was at least good enough to show up for the birth of his son Bob Marley on February 6,

1945. Just a week after Marley was born, Norval abruptly left for Kingston once again. Marley's father would ultimately perish, dying of a heart attack, when Bob was just ten years old. It wasn't easy for Marley to grow up without a father, but early on in life, he learned not to worry about what he didn't have and make the most of what he did.

Chapter One

From Farm to Trench Town

"We don't have education, we have inspiration; if I was educated I would be a damn fool."

—Bob Marley

It's said that Marley's musical career began as a little boy when his cousin gave him a homemade guitar made out of bamboo and goatskin. With such homemade instruments on hand, Marley started to imitate old Jamaican standards, banging away and singing songs with all of his might. It seems he inherited his musical talents from his mother, who was known for her fine singing voice, and his grandfather Omeriah, who played both the violin and accordion.

As much fun as little Bob was having, life for Marley's mother had meanwhile become much harder. Although Omeriah helped the struggling single mother as much as he could, she was having a hard time getting on her own two feet. It was in search of a better life for herself that she opted to head to Kingston for work while leaving her then 11-year-old son on Omeriah's farm.

Shortly thereafter, Omeriah placed Bob in the care of Amy, Cedella's sister. Marley became a real farmer at this homestead, learning to care for a whole flock of goats.

Other than his list of chores and duties, he was left with very little instruction. Left to his own accord, in his spare time Marley began to hang out with Amy's son, Sledger. He and Sledger would have riotous good times with each other. The mischief this pair wrought apparently became too great, however, because Marley was soon sent packing back to his grandfather's farm.

For the next couple of months, he would then be directly under his grandfather Omeriah's care, as it wasn't until 1957 that his mother came calling and asking for her son. By now, she had created some form of economic independence for herself, and as such, she wished to finally be able to raise her child under her own roof. Yet although she was eking out a living for herself, Cedella's economic status was not the best. She was, in fact, living in one of the most impoverished parts of Kingston, in the west-side ghetto of the city. Here in Trench Town, people lived in close proximity to the city's dumps, where sewage and all manner of filth piled up. It was this less than stellar location that Marley and his childhood friends would make famous through their music. As bad as it may have been though, Marley and his mother lived in the nicer part of the neighborhood in the government housing units, called Government Yards.

Jamaica as a whole was in flux at this time, seeking to find its identity while coming closer and closer to total independence from its former colonial taskmaster, Great Britain. During this push for independence, Jamaica developed its two main parties, the Jamaica Labour Party and the People's National Party. These two parties had long-standing disagreements from the very beginning, and unfortunately enough, violence often erupted because of this, a trend that would come to affect Marley himself later in life.

Marley was by now enrolled in the public schools of Kingston, while his mother worked hard as a domestic servant in the homes of affluent Jamaicans on the rich side of town. It is said that although Marley proved to be a good student, very shortly into his formal education, he became disillusioned with his studies. His attendance became sporadic, and by the age of 15, he stopped going to school at all. Instead of going to school, Marley preferred to stay around the neighborhood with his friends. Relaxing with his chums, he would play football on good days and make mischief on bad ones. Along with the mischief-making, it was around this time that he decided to make music.

As mentioned earlier, Marley had an aptitude for music from a young age, but back then, it was just how he occasionally passed the time. Soon he would come to look at music as a serious vocation. His interest was piqued by a local kid by the name of Neville Livingston, or as he was better known on the street, "Bunny." Bob Marley and Bunny Livingston (later known as Bunny Wailer) shared an interconnected history that seems to have begun years earlier when Cedella met Bunny's father, Thaddeus "Toddy" Livingston. The two had an affair together despite the fact that Toddy already had a wife.

At any rate, Marley began to spend long hours with Toddy's son Bunny. During these sessions, the two would practice their own versions of Jamaican standards and rock and roll covers. During these early days of collaboration, a Jamaican form of music called ska had come to prominence. Marley and Bunny absorbed everything they could about this groundbreaking new music and combined it with the blues and the rock and roll they heard emanating from the United States. Some of the American groups that had the most impact on Marley during these early days were the likes of Elvis Presley, Fats Domino, and The Drifters.

This was the backdrop of Bob Marley's youth in Trench Town, and it was from this template that he would soon begin to fashion anthems and ballads of his own. In the past, he had merely looked to music as a hobby, but now with his friend Bunny at his side, he would soon come to consider it a very serious vocation.

Chapter Two

Marley's First Songs

"Possession make you rich? I don't have that type of richness. My richness is life, forever."

—Bob Marley

Even as Marley was expressing greater interest in living the life of a musician, his mother was becoming increasingly alarmed that her son was unemployed and seemingly drifting aimlessly in life. It was out of concern for his future and what career he might take that she convinced Marley to take a position at a local welding shop. Marley wasn't too thrilled about the job, but seeing as his friend Desmond Dekker was already an employee, he reluctantly accepted the position.

Just like Marley, Dekker was a budding musician who would come to find success on the reggae music scene. Dekker encouraged Marley to keep developing his musical talents, and the two would trade thoughts and ideas in that regard while on the job.

Around the same time, Marley met another young musician by the name of Peter McIntosh (known by the locals as Peter Tosh). Peter was into a lot of the same music that Marley and Bunny were into, and—even more appealing—he owned a guitar, which was a rare commodity in Marley's circle of friends. It was on this guitar, with Peter's guidance, that Bob Marley first learned the instrument.

Soon enough, the three of them, Bob, Bunny, and Tosh, were regularly performing together. As their musical acumen grew, Marley became increasingly disinterested in his day job as a welder, and when he had an accident in the shop and a piece of metal shot up in his eye, he decided to quit. The metal was eventually taken out, but Marley never went back on the job. His mother was certainly disappointed with his decision since, to most outside observers, it seemed rather unwise to give up a valuable tradecraft like welding for the typically unprofitable business of music. Yet Marley and company would soon prove just how lucrative their music could be.

They formed a group that would soon come under the guidance of a man who was already a legend—Joe Higgs. Higgs was part of the hitmaking group Higgs and Wilson and was beloved by the community. Luckily, he was also more than willing to give that love back by mentoring up-and-coming local talent such as Marley and his friends, helping them improve their skills. Higgs tutored the group and taught them how to harmonize better.

By the early 1960s, Marley had become interested in creating songs as a solo artist. He managed to gain some recording time in the studio with a local guru named Leslie Kong, and these efforts resulted in the singles "One Cup of Coffee," "Judge Not," "Do You Still Love Me?" and "Terror," which were all completed in early 1962. Marley was only 16 years old at the time that he cut these singles, and even though they didn't get much traction, just the fact that he had put his work out there for public consumption was an achievement in itself. Long before the days when just about anyone could self-promote themselves on social media, Marley having the opportunity to record his work in a studio was a big deal.

The song "Judge Not" was perhaps the most quintessentially Marley song at the time, with its admonition for others not to judge him unless they first "judged themselves." The song was full of the rich philosophy that would later come to guide so much of his life, and although the songs were not much of a commercial success, Bob Marley's career had officially begun.

Chapter Three

Topping the Charts in Jamaica

"Truth is—everybody is going to hurt you. You just got to find the ones worth suffering for."

—Bob Marley

Just as Marley was making some inroads in the music business, growing drama in his family was threatening to make it all come undone. His mother Cedella had been in an ongoing relationship with Bunny's father—a relationship which eventually yielded a baby girl. In the complicated web that was woven, Marley and his friend Bunny now shared a little sister named Pearl, while Marley's mother was still little more than the mistress of Bunny's father.

Shortly after the birth of Pearl, Mr. Livingston broke it off with Cedella for good. She then left in a hurry and made a trip all the way to Delaware, on the East Coast of the United States. Cedella had some relatives in the area and intended to stay with them for a while. It remains unclear if she expected Marley to join her, but it seems he was determined to stay in Jamaica whether his mother was there or not.

Marley had just turned 18 at the time and was already on his own. Without a permanent residence, he went from one friend's house to another. A true starving artist, he often sang for his supper, playing music just to eke out a meager, barely self-sustaining existence.

It was in these dark and uncertain times that Marley decided to give up on being a solo artist for the time being and re-join his bandmates. He received news meanwhile in late 1962 that his mother had already met and married another man. She wed an American named Edward Booker, thereby gaining residency for herself. It seems that she intended to have her son join her at this point, but Marley—not willing to leave his bandmates behind—must have declined the invitation. He was busy crafting what would become his first hit—an anthem-styled song called "Simmer Down."

This song dealt with the growing tension among the young people in the poorer regions of Jamaica. The song advises the listener to "simmer down" and keep a lid on aggression. Jamaica had just gained its official independence from Britain in July of 1962, and over the next few years, many of the political factions in Jamaica would be vying for power. It was in this vein that a young Bob Marley sought to encourage his peers to dial down the temperature. Marley using his voice as a calming salve during times of intensity would be a recurring theme throughout his career.

By the time Marley and his friends crafted "Simmer Down," they had both literally and metaphorically developed a name for themselves in Jamaica, calling themselves the Wailing Wailers. This was a musical moniker that Bob would carry in some form or other for the rest of his career.

The finished product for "Simmer Down" was introduced to the radio in late 1963, and by 1964, it had managed to reach number one on the Jamaican charts. Bob Marley and his friends were now undisputed local heroes—a feat achieved very early on in their career. Yet it would take much longer for them to receive recognition outside of Jamaica itself.

Chapter Four

Marriage and Children

"The greatness of a man is not in how much wealth he acquires, but in his integrity and his ability to affect those around him positively."

—Bob Marley

After their success with "Simmer Down," Marley and the Wailing Wailers became regulars at the studio. During this industrious period, the band recorded "It Hurts To Be Alone," "Lonesome Feeling," and the 1965 hit, "I'm Still Waiting." It was also during this time that Marley began to really develop his talent for playing the guitar. Prior to this, the group had focused on the harmonization of their voices, but now they sought to hone their instrumentation as well.

Marley and company were in the midst of all of this refinement when the group began to move away from ska to more of a rocksteady rhythm. Rocksteady is a little slower than the frenetically fast ska music and is typically viewed as a forerunner to reggae. It certainly was a time for refinement for the group, and by the end of the year, they had shed the extra studio musicians they had picked up in favor of a rawer sound, consisting of just the core founders, Bob, Bunny, and Tosh.

It was at this juncture that they dropped "Wailing" from their moniker and started to simply call themselves the

Wailers. It was also around this time that Marley met a woman that would prove to be one of the most pivotal relationships of his life. Her name was Rita Anderson. Rita, like Bob, was an aspiring singer and was seeking to gain recording time at Studio One—Marley's main base of operations.

Even at this early stage in his life, Marley had already been in relationships with several women, one of which had allegedly produced a child—a daughter by the name of Imani Carole. Not much is known about Imani or her mother, or for that matter many of the other children that Marley would father throughout his career. As one of Marley's later biographers, Richie Unterberger, once put it, "Most accounts place the number at about a dozen offspring, birthed by almost as many women."

This lack of information about all the extramarital children Marley would go on to have has made it virtually impossible for biographers to adequately document this aspect of his life. At any rate, it is believed that in 1965 when he first met Rita Anderson, Marley was already a father to Imani.

Rita also had a child at the time, a little girl named Sharon, that Marley would eventually adopt as his own. Rita was staying with her aunt and uncle when she first met Marley, and soon thereafter, she invited him to move in with her. Rita's relatives did not appreciate the extra boarder, however, and ended up moving the pair out of the house and into a makeshift shack put up in the family's backyard. It was a primitive dwelling to be sure, but it was at least a place of their own.

Marley tried to better himself financially meanwhile, and after receiving some royalties from his work in the studio, he asked Rita to marry him. The two were then duly wed on February 10, 1966. Interestingly enough, in what was seemingly an echo of what his own father had done to him, just days after he married Rita, Marley took off. He wasn't so much as abandoning his new bride, but he was taking a decidedly abrupt leave of absence. Shortly after he said "I do," Marley ventured out to visit his mother's stomping grounds in America, in the state of Delaware.

Chapter Five

Marley the Rastafari

"Be still, and know that His Imperial Majesty, Emperor Haile Selassie of Ethiopia is the Almighty."

—Bob Marley

As big of a star as Marley had become in Jamaica, he was still virtually unknown in the United States. With his band left behind on the island, he had no means of making money except to resort to menial labor. To support himself while visiting his family in Delaware, he worked as a forklift driver, parking lot attendant, and at one point even a laboratory assistant.

Strange as it may seem, upon his arrival in America, this Jamaican superstar did indeed take on some of the most menial of jobs. This is a clear demonstration of how unknown Bob Marley was outside of Jamaica. If Marley would have mentioned to his colleagues during a lunch break that he had a hit song back in his home country, no one would have believed him.

It was also around this time that Marley began to change his views on religion and took up an active interest in Rastafarianism. In later years, reggae and the cultural/religious beliefs of Rastafarianism would become so intertwined that many would have trouble separating them, but they are in fact two different things.

Rastafarianism dates back to the early 1930s when a Jamaican philosopher by the name of Leonard Howell took great inspiration from the crowning of Ethiopia's new emperor, Haile Selassie. The East African nation of Ethiopia has virtually no connection to Jamaicans who are descendants of West Africa, but the fact that Ethiopia was the only remaining independent African nation left on the continent was a source of pride for many in the African diaspora.

Ethiopia itself certainly has a rich history, with an ancient civilization directly mentioned in the Old Testament of the Bible. Haile Selassie was the last Ethiopian ruler from a line said to date back to Menelik I, the son of Israel's King Solomon and Ethiopia's Queen of Sheba. Menelik, the king of kings, ruled over a feudal kingdom with various lesser kings or governors, who directly presided over different sections of the Ethiopian Empire. The Ethiopian term for these governors was *ras*. Prior to being crowned emperor in 1930, Haile Selassie himself was a ras, ruling over a province in Eastern Ethiopia called Harar.

Back in the days when Haile Selassie governed Harar, he went by his birth name of Tafari, which made his official title Ras Tafari, or in other words, Governor Tafari. In 1930, when Leonard Howell heard of a certain Ras Tafari being crowned emperor in Ethiopia, he was so enthused about it that he managed to spark an entire religious movement around the event.

As bizarre as all this may sound, this is precisely how Rastafarianism came about. Haile Selassie himself was probably more baffled by these developments than anyone else. Selassie was after all—like most Ethiopians—a devoted Orthodox Christian, and the idea that someone would make him into a God was completely anathema to his sensibilities. For most, the beliefs of the Rastafarians are hard to comprehend, but then again, belief is a very powerful thing, and young Bob Marley was drawn to the Rastafarian faith all the same.

Interestingly enough, it was actually while Marley was away in America that Haile Selassie made his famous trip to Jamaica in 1966. For Rastafarians eager for a sign, Selassie's presence was greeted with great fanfare. Marley's wife Rita was at the event and would later claim that when she was in the crowd gathered to hear Selassie speak, she beheld a miraculous sight.

According to her, at one point when the emperor raised his hands to the crowd, she could clearly see the imprint of nails on his wrists. Rita believed that this was an indication that Selassie, just like Christ, had hung on the cross. Such beliefs fell right in line with the idea that the last emperor of Ethiopia was the second coming of Jesus Christ.

At any rate, it's clear that by the time of Selassie's trip, Rastafarianism had become all the rage in Jamaica. Even Marley's bandmates in the Wailers had become firm adherents to the faith. Without missing a beat, upon his return to Jamaica, Marley readily accepted these cultural changes of his peers. Along with adoption of Rastafarianism, Marley and his friends also started freely using marijuana, or as it is referred in Rasta circles, "ganja," as it was considered to be a gateway to enlightenment.

During this period, Marley met a man that would serve as his mentor and manager for the rest of his life, a Rastafarian elder by the name of Mortimer Planno. It was also around this time that Marley's family increased as his wife gave birth to their first child, a girl they named after Marley's mother, Cedella. Bob wanted the best for his growing family, but it was still a hardscrabble existence for the most part, and at times, they were even forced to make do through subsistence farming in between Marley's performing and recording gigs.

The Wailers meanwhile recorded several new singles, which included the Rastafari piece, "Selassie Is The Chapel," as well as "Nice Time" and the later hit, "Stir It Up." Marley and his musical cohorts, the Wailers, were ready to take the world by storm, whether the world was aware of it or not.

Chapter Six

The Birth of Reggae Music

"When one door is closed, don't you know, another is open."

—Bob Marley

By the late 1960s, the Wailers' steady rise began to slow down as issues among the band members began to impede the creative process. First, in 1968, Peter Tosh was thrown in jail, incarcerated for his participation in a political demonstration. Shortly thereafter, Bunny and Bob were both incarcerated after being found with marijuana on their person. As soon as the trio was released, however, they took the adversity they experienced and used it to fuel their creativity.

One source of happiness and joy for Marley during this period was the birth of his son David, whom he would come to nickname Ziggy, an endearing moniker that would stick with the boy for the rest of his life.

When Marley wasn't making music or spending time with his family, he was hanging out with his sometimes manager, sometimes mentor, the unabashed Rasta Mortimer Planno. Planno brought Marley down to Jones Town, where he introduced him to a particularly dedicated group of Rastas. It was through these Rasta circles that Bob met an American musician by the name of Johnny Nash.

Nash was already famous for his hit "Let's Move and Groove Together," and at this time, Nash and an associate of his by the name of Danny Sims were trying to sign Jamaican talent to their own record label. Sure enough, once Nash met Bob Marley, he figured he had struck some real musical gold.

Nash was ready to sign the group and start producing records for them, but Bunny was still incarcerated at the time. Since Bunny was very much involved in the process in those days, production would have to wait. He was eventually released from jail in the fall of 1968, and almost immediately thereafter, the old trio began making music again.

Under the JAD Records label, the group produced singles such as "Put It On," "Mellow Mood," and "There She Goes." Tempo-wise these songs fell into the rocksteady moderate beat, but shortly thereafter, rocksteady itself began to change. Musicians were suddenly playing everything in a slowed-down groove that they called reggae. It was a sound that was made famous in 1968 by the likes of Toots and the Maytals with their smash hit "Do the Reggay."

Bob Marley and company, who were already heading in that direction, were quick to catch on and soon adopted the sounds of reggae for their own music. Feeling greatly inspired, the group went back to Studio One, and with the help of their old producer Leslie Kong, they recorded new reggae styled grooves, such as "Stop That Train," "Go Tell It On The Mountain," "Soul Shakedown Party," "Can't You See," "Cheer Up," and "Do It Twice."

The songs were released by Kong as singles, but unfortunately for Marley, they all failed to catch on. In order to salvage what must have seemed like a complete loss, Kong then attempted to recoup by putting some of the songs on a greatest hits piece entitled *The Best of the Wailers*.

This was very upsetting to Marley and his bandmates. For one thing, the songs had all received a decidedly negative reception, so it almost seemed like cruel sarcasm on the part of Kong to put these commercial flops together and call them "The Best of the Wailers." To Marley and company, this seemed tantamount to mockery. As such, the group demanded that Kong cease and desist, yet an unmoved Leslie Kong went ahead and issued the greatest hits album regardless.

For Kong, this was the last major project he would work on since shortly thereafter, he abruptly perished from heart failure. He was only 37 years old. Some claimed that Marley, who as a child had supposedly dabbled in the "dark arts," had perhaps placed a hex on Kong in his anger. Of course, there is no evidence any such thing ever happened. At any rate, as was typically the case in Bob Marley's life, as soon as one door came to a close, another was just getting ready to open.

Chapter Seven
Commercial Success

"Don't trust people whose feelings change with time. Trust people whose feelings remain the same, even when the time changes."

—Bob Marley

After it was all said and done, Bob Marley found himself a little bit disillusioned in 1969, so much so that he decided to take a break from the music business and once again pay a visit to his mother in the United States. While there, he took up some manual labor jobs, which sadly enough paid more than the meager royalties he had thus far received for his music.

It was the paychecks he earned from working at a Chrysler automobile plant while staying with his mother that Marley would take back to Jamaica to help support his family over the next few months. It must have been sad to have to struggle like this and yet be so close to making it big, but Marley pushed on regardless.

Shortly thereafter, Marley took his bandmates to Studio One to work on a new round of songs. For this series of recordings, the group was given a rawer feel, and the songs featured more driving bass and percussion. On the heels of these successful recordings, around 1970, the group created their own record label called Tuff Gong. It was actually based on a nickname Marley had developed as a youth in Trench Town. Rastafarian founder Leonard Howell had been known as "The Gong," and somehow or other, Marley was jokingly referred to by his colleagues as "Tuff Gong."

At any rate, no matter what they called the new record label project, it failed to take off. For a time, the group seemed to be going around in circles. They would drop singles, gain some traction, but then inevitably find themselves back at square one. Luckily, their next breakthrough would come in 1972 when Marley and the Wailers went back into the studio and produced an album called *Catch a Fire*. The phrase "catch a fire" was actually a Jamaican slang phrase that meant that someone was "asking for trouble" or "catching hell." This album boasted the fully formed reggae anthems "Stop That Train," "Concrete Jungle," "Kinky Reggae," "No More Trouble," and "Stir It Up."

The album featured the core group of Bob Marley, Bunny Wailer, and Peter Tosh, as well as session musicians such as Aston and Carlie Barrett. Once the songs were put down on tape, Marley sent them off to London to have them further mixed and mastered. This led to some pretty heavy guitar overdubs by British guitarist Wayne Perkins and keyboardist John Bundrick.

The additional flourishes dubbed over the original recordings after the fact were intended to give the music a more rock-driven feel that would appeal to wider audiences outside of Jamaica. The formula seemed to work because finally, with the release of *Catch a Fire*, the outside world seemed to catch on to reggae and the work of Bob Marley.

Along with the release of this bold new album, Marley celebrated the birth of an additional child, a son named Stephen. Realizing that his expanding family needed some more space, Marley decided to move his wife and kids away from Kingston proper and to a new place, an enclave in Bull Bay, some ten miles east of the Jamaican capital.

This was a major move for Marley since it was the first time that he was able to lift his family out of the poverty of Kingston's slums and begin to live a more prosperous life. Unfortunately for his wife, it also marked the moment that Bob Marley began a long litany of affairs with other women. As mentioned earlier, he would end up fathering several children with other women throughout his life.

Marley's dalliances with other women had become little more than an open secret at this point, and although Rita would stay with him until his death, she most certainly knew that her husband was not faithful. Something that he was always faithful to, though, was his Rastafarian ideals and his commitment to improving the political situation in Jamaica.

During this time, Marley became involved with one of the main political parties on the island—the PNP, or People's National Party. He supported the PNP's candidate Michael Manley in the 1972 election for prime minister and was overjoyed when he successfully won the position. As much as Marley was thrilled at his election, the rival party—the Jamaican Labour Party (JLP)—was not, and the fact that Bob Marley was such a vocal supporter for the PNP would not be forgotten. This support would, in fact, one day come back to haunt Marley in a very dramatic way.

Chapter Eight

The Wailers Break Up

"The people who were trying to make this world worse are not taking the day off. Why should I?"

—Bob Marley

In the spring of 1973, Bob Marley and the Wailers started touring for their new album *Catch a Fire*. The first leg of the tour began in Great Britain, where they performed at a total of 19 different venues. They also showed up as special guests on BBC variety shows such as *Top Gear* and *The Old Grey Whistle Test*.

Bunny meanwhile had become ill during their visit to the U.K. although some sources contend that the illness was a ruse and that he simply didn't feel like going out on tour. Whatever the case may be, upon their return to Jamaica, Bunny announced that he didn't intend to go with them when they picked up their tour again in the United States.

This was a critical juncture for the band and to have such a crucial member of the core of the group decide to suddenly sit things out was nerve-racking to say the least. Nevertheless, the group was determined to go on—with or without Bunny at their side. They didn't have to look far for a replacement, as they managed to recruit their old mentor Joe Higgs. Upon their arrival in America, their first gigs would be to sell-out crowds in Boston and New York, which included a stint that had them sharing the stage with none other than "The Boss" himself—Bruce Springsteen.

It must have been a feeling of vindication for Bob Marley to return to the East Coast where he had labored as a forklift driver just a few years earlier. Before this star could truly go supernova, however, there were still a few things he needed to learn.

According to the later recollection of Bunny's fill-in, Joe Higgs, the group was good, but still in a transitional phase. They were finding their footing and seeking the best way to connect with a larger audience. Standing up on stage and looking out at the crowd, Higgs noted that the sound that they brought "was something they weren't ready to accept immediately."

As far as they had come, Marley and company decided that their sound needed just a little more refinement. So it was, as soon as they got back from Jamaica, they put together a much more expansive follow-up, which they called *Burnin'*. This album, whose cover featured a silhouette of the six core Wailers' heads burned into the side of a wooden box, was much more political in nature, focusing on social issues and Rastafarian philosophy.

The album featured such powerful renditions as "Rasta Man Chant," "I Shot the Sheriff," "Get Up, Stand Up," and "One Foundation." Shortly after this album was released, the group went on another tour of the United States, this time performing alongside the Funkadelic American band Sly and the Family Stone. Bunny once again chose to sit the tour out and was replaced by Joe Higgs.

At first, it seemed like a great opportunity for the band to get more exposure, since Sly and the Family Stone was a well-known and popular group at the time. Sadly, the tour proved to be short-lived, with the Wailers being dismissed after only four performances. Marley and his compatriots apparently rubbed Sly the wrong way and were accused of trying to upstage them.

Not only were Marley and the Wailers accused of outplaying the headliners, but it was also suggested that the audience just didn't vibe with their music. It was a frustrating rejection to be sure, and one that left Marley and the band stranded right in the middle of Las Vegas. It was in the desert of Nevada that the Wailers were given the boot, leaving Marley to figure out what to do next.

Seeking to salvage what was left of their time in the United States, Marley managed to get some gigs in California, including a packed venue in San Francisco at a night club called the Matrix. Spurned and rejected, at this memorable concert, Bob Marley was said to have been rather intense to behold. As one reporter for the *San Francisco Chronicle* described it at the time, "Marley, songwriter, bandleader and leader singer, bobs up and down, wavering in front of the microphone—very high and stoned—completely oblivious to the mike. He breaks all the rules of microphone technique—looking away and down at the same time even—yet his pitch is pure and unfaltering."

The group also appeared live on the local radio station KSAN-FM around this time, performing impromptu renditions of songs such as "Rasta Man Chant" live on the air. Many have credited the appearance at the Matrix and this intriguing radio broadcast as having more to do with the creation of Marley's American fan base than anything else.

After Marley and company finished their American tour, they then made a brief pit stop back in Jamaica before preparing to head across the Atlantic to perform in Great Britain. Higgs himself would pull out this time and declined to travel with the group, leaving Marley and Peter Tosh to go on without him.

Without Higgs, the band got off to a rough start and failed to garner much interest from the British. Under the stress of a series of bad gigs, things got so bad that frustrations boiled over enough one night that Bob Marley and Peter Tosh got into a fist fight. This proved to be the end of the Wailers, leaving Marley to pick up the pieces as best he could.

Chapter Nine

No Woman, No Cry

"Just because you are happy it does not mean that the day is perfect but that you have looked beyond its imperfections."

—Bob Marley

In early 1974, Marley found himself back in Kingston and back to the drawing board as far as his musical career was concerned. With his former bandmates bailing on him, he focused on creating new songs on his own. Even though the original Wailers were gone, Marley picked up some other studio musicians and continued to use the Wailers name.

Still, the old trio of Bob, Bunny, and Tosh would at least have one more last hurrah before they went their separate ways. The occasion came when they were tapped to be the opening act for the famed American rhythm and blues crooner Marvin Gaye. Marley and the Wailers didn't have to go to America for this concert, as Gaye came to Jamaica for a benefit concert. The concert proved to be enormously successful, but no matter how good it may have been, it still wasn't enough to convince Bunny and Tosh to remain, and the three musicians that had been through so much together decided to go their separate ways for good.

As such, Marley went back to the studio and cobbled together whatever studio musicians he could and forged ahead with his new album, *Natty Dread*. One of the most notable changes was the use of an electronic drum beat, rather than a live studio drummer. Although an electro beat would become common by the late 1970s with the rise of disco music, this was still rather uncommon during the first half of the decade.

Besides the innovation of an electronic beat, *Natty Dread* had a similar feel to earlier Bob Marley songs, with rich and soulful tunes such as "So Jah She" and "No Woman, No Cry." But the song that would really prove a breakthrough for Marley in 1974 was "I Shot The Sherriff." It wasn't Marley's rendition that would become famous at first, but rather Eric Clapton's. Guitar guru Clapton gained permission from Marley to record his own version, and his jammed-out rendition managed to top the charts.

In the end though, it was "No Woman, No Cry" that would prove to be the real breakthrough for Marley as he released his *Live!* album in 1975. The recordings themselves were compiled from concerts that Marley had performed in Britain that summer. Indeed, many concert goers had noted that Marley's magic was more evident during live concerts rather than studio sessions.

As one music critic put it at the time, "The band are solid and unified, gliding more than steamrollering, and they keep coming; never more so than on 'Lively Up Yourself,' which was so powerful that it made the recorded version seem positively Mickey Mouse by comparison."

But of course, it was the ultimate hit of "No Woman, No Cry" that elicited the greatest praise from the audience.

Initially, the *Live!* album was only released in Europe, but the few imports that made it to the United States sold well, convincing the label to issue a full release in America as well. This success was then followed up by the release of *Rastaman Vibration* in the summer of 1976.

Now that the wider world had finally been introduced to Bob Marley, they couldn't get enough, and his latest album soon scored high on the charts. Songs like "War," "Positive Vibration," and "Night Shift" were some of the most memorable.

"Night Shift" was as interesting as it was honest in its reflections of when—not too long ago—Bob Marley worked the night shift at an automotive plant in Delaware, driving a forklift. Most notably though, it was "Rastaman Vibration" that had Marley recommitting himself to his Rastafarian beliefs—a feat much harder for Rastafarians to do in the aftermath of their idol Haile Selassie's death in 1975.

As much as Jamaicans had grown to love Haile Selassie, a simmering unrest had been growing among Selassie's own people in Ethiopia. A terrible famine had struck the country in 1973, and student agitators and communist sympathizers used this calamity and past grievances to spark an insurrection against the emperor's rule. Selassie was arrested by Ethiopian communist militants called the Derg in 1974 and was killed on August 27, 1975.

The news of Selassie's death was obviously disruptive for Rastafarians since they viewed the man as a manifestation of God. This led some to rethink their previous beliefs, but others still held firm—Bob Marley among them. Marley refused to believe that Selassie was dead, and his song "Jah Live" bore testament to his belief that Selassie was still alive. Rastafarians often referred to Selassie as "Jah." In the song, Marley insisted that Jah was still alive and he was going to "scatter his enemies."

Unfortunately for Ethiopia, Haile Selassie's main enemy, Mengistu Haile Mariam, wasn't going anywhere anytime soon. In the next few years, he would transform Ethiopia into a dictatorial nightmare that would not end until he was finally deposed in 1991.

Chapter Ten

The Assassination Attempt

"God sent me on Earth. He send me to do something, and nobody can stop me. If God want to stop me, then I stop. Man never can."

—Bob Marley

The Rastaman tour began in earnest in April of 1976 and would send Marley on an extensive run across America and Europe. His first concert of the tour was held in Pennsylvania at the Tower Theatre. One of the most interesting things about this concert was the fact that Marley's mother Cedella, who had been living on America's East Coast for several years by then, finally took the opportunity to see her son perform live in concert.

After this milestone was made, Marley went off to play at several more gigs on the East Coast before crossing the border to Canada, where he performed in Toronto and Montreal. He then double-backed to the United States to play shows in Buffalo, New York, and Cleveland, Ohio. From Ohio, he then charged right through the Midwest, only to turn south and head all the way down to Texas.

After Texas, Marley went west and made an appearance at seven different venues in California. One of these venues—the Roxy Theatre in Hollywood—had none other than that the other famous Bob—Bob Dylan—in the audience. Marley was said to have greatly admired the folk singer, and this rising star of reggae was sure to play it up for the veteran. Marley finally ended his breakneck speed tour of the U.S. by showing up in Miami, Florida. From here, the group disembarked for Europe, where they performed at various locales in Wales, France, Holland, Germany, and Sweden.

After this heady tour came to a close, Marley came back to Jamaica for a much-needed rest. He couldn't rest for long, however, since Prime Minister Michael Manley was right in the middle of his re-election campaign. Political fever was in the air, and it wasn't long before Marley was swept into the middle of it. The two political parties vying for power, the PNP and the JLP, had become so hostile toward each other that their respective supporters seemed on the verge of pitching the entire country into a civil war.

Marley, growing increasingly alarmed, sought to soothe the situation with whatever influence he could muster from his superstar status. He proposed a concert called Smile Jamaica. It remains unclear exactly what Marley wanted his audience to smile about, but it was a gathering that was meant to foster a general feeling of peace and love.

Prior to hosting such a festivity, Marley had to get permission from Jamaica's prime minister, Michael Manley himself. Marley requested the date for the concert to be on December 5, 1976, and conveniently, the general election would be held less than two weeks later. This coupled with the fact that Marley had supported the People's National Party in the past made it seem like the concert was more of a political "get out the vote rally" for Prime Minister Manley than anything else.

This interpretation of events would lead to Marley becoming a target of angry JLP fanatics. Just a couple of days prior to the scheduled concert, Marley and his bandmates were practicing at Marley's house when armed assailants suddenly barged in and began shooting. The altercation occurred in the kitchen, and Marley managed to duck behind a refrigerator, shielding him from many of the bullets.

His manager Don Taylor, however, wasn't as lucky, having been caught by the gunmen right in the middle of the melee and was said to have been "riddled with bullets." After opening fire, the gunmen fled the scene. Marley received injuries to his arm and torso, but Don Taylor's condition was obviously much more severe. Miraculously enough, after being airlifted to a hospital, Taylor received an emergency operation that would save his life.

With this attack, it was clear that extremists from JLP were trying to make sure that Marley did not hold his Smile Jamaica concert. Yet if they thought they could deter Marley with their aggression, they had another thing coming. Marley held the concert just as he had planned, striding across the stage in front of a roaring crowd at Jamaica's National Heroes Park on December 5. His playing was as passionate and frenetic as usual, but the most powerful moment of the night was when he addressed the audience directly.

As hundreds of people gathered round, Marley displayed his arm where his intended hitman had shot him just days before and declared, "Bang-bang—I'm okay."

The crowd roared with delight, yet curiously stayed around him like a living wall, lest any further gunmen might try to get at their idol. With their rapt attention, Marley then explained to the audience, "When I decided to do this concert two and a half months ago, there were no politicians involved. I just wanted to play for the love of the people." Even though some had tried to present Marley as a political hack, Marley wanted to make it clear that he was not performing for political reasons.

Shortly after the concert, Marley hopped on a plane and headed to Nassau in the Bahamas to record some songs at his friend and producer Chris Blackwell's Compass Point Studios. This was considered a safehouse for Marley where he was able to tend his wounds and plan his next move. Jamaica's general election took place as planned meanwhile, and Prime Minister Manley was successfully re-elected.

Marley lingered in Nassau for a bit before he and his bandmates moved on to Great Britain. After Marley arrived in London, he and his crew acquired a rental in the Chelsea district and set up shop. It was shortly after the dawning of 1977 that Marley went into the studio to record what would become his next masterpiece work, entitled *Exodus*. It was a very apt title for this refugee since he had indeed been forced to make a rapid exodus from Jamaica.

Exodus was released that summer and proved to be a masterpiece, staying high on the British charts for several weeks in a row. The album seemed to capture Bob Marley's state of mind—hopeful, yet reflective of what had happened to him. The first track, was a piece called "Natural Mystic." It just so happened that "Natural Mystic" was one of the pet names that Bob's associates called him by, and in many ways, the song itself was said to serve as a herald to his return to writing new music.

Many of the other songs were typical Rasta anthems, calling for unity and resolve in the face of oppression. The last half of the album then evolved into feel good tunes such as "Jamming," "Turn Your Lights Down Low," and "One Love," the latter of which would prove to be one of Bog Marley's biggest hit songs of all time.

Soon after *Exodus* was released, the band went out on tour in support of it. As was usually the case, the tour would have them crisscrossing both America and Europe. Just prior to setting out, however, Marley managed to get pulled over by the police. During the traffic stop, the cops found marijuana, which then gave them incentive to search Marley's London flat. Despite the fact that the police found about a pound of marijuana at Marley's residence, he managed to escape with just a warning and a small fine.

After arriving in Paris, France in the summer of 1977, Marley's tour began in earnest. He blazed a path through France to Belgium, Holland, Germany, and Denmark. By July, he was setting course for the United States, which turned into one of his most successful tours of all time.

Once Marley wrapped up his tour in America, he finally made his return to Jamaica. Unfortunately, by this time, Jamaica had become even more politically unstable. Manley had won re-election, but his opposition had become even more vocal and volatile than ever. It was so bad in fact that Manley had declared martial law and sent out the troops just to keep some semblance of the peace.

It was in this incredibly tumultuous backdrop that Marley hosted the One Love Peace Concert. On April 22, 1978, at the National Stadium in Kingston, Marley and his bandmates took the stage in an attempt to use the power of their music to heal the wounds of the nation. Bob Marley headlined the event with several other smaller acts playing in support.

In the build-up for the concert, Marley managed to produce and release a brand new album of all new material called *Kaya*. Although the album had several memorable songs, it has often been lambasted by critics as being too commercialized and straying away from Marley's roots.

At any rate, for the One Love Peace Concert, when Marley and company took the stage, tens of thousands of fans were in attendance. They expected much from the reggae superstar, and Bob Marley did not disappoint. He ended up playing for about an hour, with extended variations of hit songs such as "Positive Vibration," "Trench Town Rock," and of course, "One Love."

The most memorable moment of the concert came in the midst of the song "Jamming." While the band jammed, Marley began what started out as a random tribute to the late Haile Selassie, which ultimately turned into a call for Prime Minister Michael Manley and opposition leader of the JLP, Edward Seaga—both of whom were in attendance—to get on stage and make amends.

Marley stunned the audience when he requested, "I'm trying to say, could we have, could we have, up here on stage. . . . The presence of Mr. Michael Manley and Mr. Edward Seaga. I just want to shake hands and show the people that we're gonna unite."

Incredibly enough, with the pressure on, both Manley and Seaga got up and headed toward the stage to heed Marley's call. Both men stood before him on the platform as Marley grabbed each man by the hand before bringing the two men's hands together in what was meant to be a show of solidarity and unity despite party differences.

It's certainly debatable how much of a difference the One Love Peace Concert made when it came to bringing actual peace to Jamaica, but regardless of the results, this iconic moment lives on as one of the greatest in Jamaican history.

Conclusion

The final years of Bob Marley's life were busy ones. In 1979, he released an album entitled *Survival*, which was filled with several reggae anthems about standing strong in the face of oppression. One of the most notable tracks was the song "Zimbabwe," which was a call for the independence of the African region of Rhodesia. This part of the world would indeed gain independence and would eventually become the modern nation of Zimbabwe under Robert Mugabe. In one of the strange ironies of Bob Marley's life, it would be Zimbabwe and its long-time leader Robert Mugabe that would shelter Mengistu Haile Mariam—the dictator that took over Ethiopia after Haile Selassie's death—after he was deposed in 1991. Mengistu lives in Zimbabwe to this day despite having been convicted of genocide by the Ethiopian government.

Close on the heels of *Survivor*, Marley released his follow-up album, *Uprising*, in 1980. This would be the last album produced in his lifetime. This work would contain some of his most powerful songs, such as "Forever Loving Jah" and "Redemption Song."

It was shortly after *Uprising* was released that Marley's health began to take a turn for the worse. He had run himself ragged with virtually non-stop touring and recording for the last few years of his life, and he seemed near exhaustion. By the time of the American leg of the *Uprising* tour in the fall of 1980, it was clear that something was wrong. Marley was often sick in bed, and then one day whilst taking a jog in Central Park in New York, he fell to the ground and went into convulsions.

A friend who was with him at the time managed to get Marley back to his hotel, where he managed to recoup, but it would prove to be just a brief respite. Shortly thereafter, Marley finally broke down and went to see a doctor. An examination revealed that the reggae star was riddled with cancer. Marley had been diagnosed with a type of skin cancer as early as 1977, after which he had the nail and nail bed of one of his toes removed in the hopes that this would be enough to combat the illness. Unfortunately, after his collapse in 1980, it was discovered that the cancer had continued to spread throughout his body.

Marley was as devastated as anyone would be, but he wasn't going to give up without a fight. He tried a vigorous round of alternative medicine to see if there was some way to get well. In these efforts, he went all the way to Germany to the Sunshine House Cancer Clinic to be treated by the controversial Dr. Josef Issels.

Issels believed that a more holistic approach was needed to treat cancer, and he championed the idea of boosting the immune system in order to fight the illness. This had him advising patients to take on very specific diets and other healthcare regimens. Marley did just as he was asked, but after a few months, it was clear that he was only getting worse.

Wishing to be back home, he boarded a plane for Jamaica. During the flight, his condition became so bad that after disembarking in Miami, Florida, he was rushed straight to the hospital. He struggled and fought valiantly, but Bob Marley would ultimately pass away on May 11, 1981, aged 36. He was gone, but his legend will never die.

Bibliography

Farley, Christopher (2007). *Before the Legend: The Rise of Bob Marley.*

Goldman, Vivien (2006). *The Book of Exodus: The Making and Meaning of Bob Marley and the Wailers' Album of the Century.*

Gooden, Lou (2003). *Reggae Heritage: Jamaica's Music History, Culture & Politic.*

Marley, Rita; Jones, Hettie (2004). *No Woman No Cry: My Life with Bob Marley.*

Moskowitz, David (2007). *Bob Marley: A Biography.*

Salewicz, Chris (2009). *Bob Marley: The Untold Story.*

Unterberger, Richie (2017). *Bob Marley and the Wailers: The Ultimate Illustrated History.*

Printed in Great Britain
by Amazon